the summer bucket list for kids

Michelle Snow

RN MSPH MSHR PhD

illustrations by
Melissa Bastow

60 fun-filled activities and crafts

the summer bucket list for kids

Michelle Snow
RN MSPH MSHR PhD

illustrations by
Melissa Bastow

plain sight publishing

an imprint of cedar fort, inc.

springville, utah

ISBN 13: 978-1-59955-484-6

Published by Plain Sight Publishing, an imprint of Cedar Fort, Inc.
2373 W. 700 S., Springville, UT, 84663
 Distributed by Cedar Fort, Inc., www.cedarfort.com

LIBRARY OF CONGRESS CATALOGING IN PUBLICATION DATA

Snow, Michelle, 1961-
 Summer bucket list for kids / Michelle Snow.
   pages cm
 ISBN 978-1-59955-484-6
 1. Amusements. 2. Creative activities and seat work. I. Title.

 GV1203.S638 2012
 793--dc23

                    2011044844

Cover design by Danie Romrell
Cover design © 2012 by Lyle Mortimer
Edited and typeset by Emily S. Chambers
Illustrated by Melissa Bastow

Printed in the United States of America

10 9 8 7 6 5 4 3 2 1

acknowledgments

To my parents, Mick Garbett and Dianne Veinotte, because they loved me enough to give me their time. And to my children, Rachel and Adam, because being their mother has given me happy memories and joy beyond measure!

Contents

Preface

My life has been filled with interesting experiences, happy associations, and desirable accomplishments. I have lived my life to its fullest measure. Through the years I have discovered the secret for satisfaction and lasting joy. Joy does not come through recognition and awards, educational degrees, national and international speaking opportunities, exotic travel destinations, and impressive careers. These are all good; but, they have not provided me with lasting satisfaction and joy. I would describe the impact of these events on my life in terms of a fleeting sense of accomplishment and momentary happiness. So what is it that has given me a lasting sense of true accomplishment and joy? Simply stated, being actively engaged in the lives of my children! Bar none, actively participating in my children's lives is the only activity that has given me lasting satisfaction and joy throughout my life. However, this did not come without a price. The price I paid was choosing to take some time away from all of the pressing matters of adult life and give that time to my children.

I desire that close friends, aunts, uncles, grandparents, and parents will take the time necessary to enjoy and enrich the lives of children through the activities found in *The Summer Bucket List for Kids*. It is my wish that as you grow old the memories of your life will be satisfying and filled with supernal joy!

Introduction

A *bucket list is typically a list of activities that* one desires to accomplish before marrying, dying or, in the case of this book, transitioning from childhood into adulthood. Over the years many friends have asked about my childhood and my experiences as a mother. I have shared with them the fun and inexpensive activities I participated in as a child as well as the memorable activities I enjoyed with my children. To my surprise most people have forgotten or never experienced many of the activities that defined my youth and parental experiences. Because of this repeated observation, I have written *The Summer Bucket List For Kids* so that these creative, educational, inexpensive, and fun activities will not be forgotten and, more importantly, so that generations of parents and children will make lasting memories together. Let the fun begin!

! WARNING: Some of the activities in this book require sharp objects, fire, or substances that may be harmful if misused or improperly handled. This is NOT a children's book! This is a book that contains fun activities that REQUIRE adult participation and constant supervision.

what you will need:

1 white raw egg

1 straight pin or sewing needle

dry wall repair spackle

paper and pen

directions:

1. Select a raw, white egg.

2. With a pin or sewing needle, carefully remove just enough of the eggshell so that a rolled up secret message can be inserted through the opening and into the egg.

3. Holding your finger over the opening that you just made, take the pin and poke a very small hole in the opposite end.

4. Covering both holes with your fingers, shake the egg vigorously. This breaks up the insides of the egg so that it will come out easier.

5. Place the egg over a bowl and blow into the smaller of the two holes. The

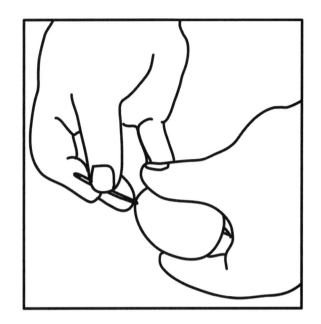

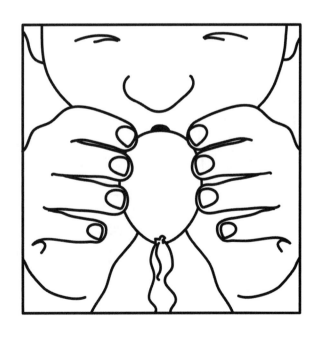

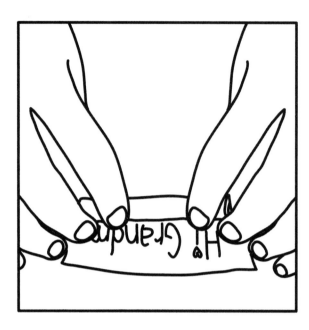

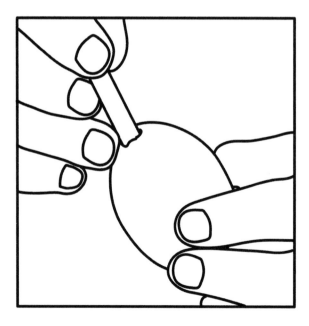

egg contents will fall out of the large hole and into the bowl.

6. Rinse the egg thoroughly, inside and out.

7. Place the egg on a paper towel and allow to dry overnight.

8. Write your secret message. Roll it up and insert it into the egg through the larger hole.

9. Remove spackle lid and stir until smooth and creamy in appearance. Smear a dab of spackle over both of the holes you made.

10. Lightly blend the spackle to match the texture of the egg shell. I use my finger. Sometimes you will need to apply two coats. Be sure to allow the first coat to dry before applying the second coat.

11. Allow to dry overnight.

12. Place the secret message egg into the egg carton with the regular eggs. Can you tell which egg is the secret egg?

One night, when i was a little girl, I was taking my bath and I got to thinking about the irrigation ditch that ran out in front of our house. I also happened to notice that the soap bar was floating on top of the water. The next morning I decided to take a bar of soap, make a mast with a bamboo skewer, and make a sail from paper. By the time I was finished, I had a great little boat. I then decided to carve the soap into different shapes to determine if I could get it to sail faster down the ditch. I tried different shaped sails and different lengths of skewer for the mast. I also tried making paper boats and boats made out of sticks and leaves.

A few days later mom brought me a cherry popsicle, my absolute favorite flavor in the world, and as I sat looking at my soap boat, I decided that I would save my popsicle sticks and when I had enough I would make popsicle stick boats. Soon my younger brother wanted to join in and we had a lot of fun racing our boats down the ditch.

I am not going to spoil your fun by telling you which materials worked best. That's something you are going to have fun figuring out for yourself!

what you will need:

old or not-being-used book (thicker is better)

clear-drying, water-soluble glue

paintbrush

a piece of thin cardboard or cardstock

a box cutter

directions:

1. Ask a parent for permission to make a secret book. They may have a special book for you to use. If not, you can buy books at library book sales or at thrift stores for $1.00-$3.00.

2. Select how many pages into the book you would like your hollow compartment to begin. In order to separate the book pages from the secret compartment, place a piece of cardboard or cardstock in-between the two sections. This will mark where to glue and where not to glue.

3. Carefully paint the outside surfaces

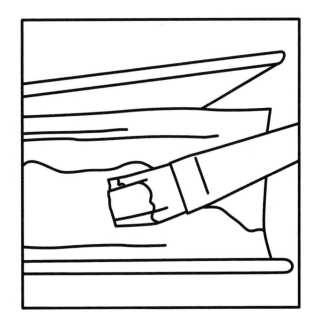

of the secret compartment pages below the cardboard with glue. Be sure to paint glue on all three outer sides of the book. Be careful to NOT paint glue on the pages above the secret compartment.

4. After painting all three outer sides of the book, place something heavy on top of the book while the glue dries.

5. When the glue is dry ask an adult to help you cut with a box cutter the shape of your secret compartment. You may want to sketch out your design on the first page. DO NOT cut all of your pages out of the bottom of your secret book or your treasures will fall out. I usually leave ¼ - ½ inch of pages on the bottom.

! Hint: Don't try to cut too many pages at once or you may end up with a sloping secret compartment.

6. Paint the inside walls of your secret compartment with glue and allow it to dry. When the glue is dry, fill your secret book with your treasures!

You may have heard that common acidic household ingredients such as milk or lemon juice can be used for invisible ink. I have tried these solutions but was unhappy with the results because more often than not, in order to get the message to appear with sufficient quality, after heat-treating the paper, I would need to apply a heavier amount of "invisible ink" which caused rippling. This was not acceptable because a clever person would see the rippling and know that something had been painted on the paper. In my quest to find an invisible ink that didn't ripple the paper, I decided to have a little fun in my kitchen trying out different common non-toxic household solutions.

Before i turned my kitchen into a laboratory I sat down and thought about what characteristics I wanted my invisible ink to possess. First, my invisible ink could not show any signs of application (such as rippling the paper). Second, the heat treatment must be at a low temperature for a short period of time. And third, the message lettering, once heat-treated, needed to become dark enough to be easily read.

If you are the type of child i was, you are probably wondering why the juice variety of invisible ink needs to be heat-treated to become visible. Here is a brief explanation:

Everything has a ph (potential for hydrogen ion concentration) value. A substance can be an acid, a base, or if it is in the middle, such as pure water, it is neutral. On the Ph scale, acids have low numbers, neutral is a 7, and bases have high numbers. Both acids and bases can be corrosive; they just react to substances differently. You might be surprised to learn that your body produces various acids and bases too. For instance, the digestive liquids in your stomach are very acidic with a Ph around 1. The juices that your pancreas secrets which break down the fatty foods you eat have a Ph of 8. This tells you that pancreatic juices are a base. Human tears on the other hand are neutral with a Ph around 7.

Let's use lemon juice for our example. Lemons have a Ph a little above 2. This means they are an acid. The lemon juice, when applied to the paper, slightly corrodes the paper. When heat is applied, the message on the paper turns brown because the acid has weakened the paper which causes the message to burn at a lower temperature.

If you are bored and need something fun to do on a rainy day, with your parent's permission, experiment with various acids and bases found in your pantry or refrigerator. You just might be surprised at the Ph of the commonly eaten foods and you may also discover a perfect invisible ink!

what you will need:

pickle juice

paintbrush or cotton swab

sheet of white paper

radiator, oven, or lightbulb

directions:

1. Write your secret message with the pickle juice using a paint brush or a cotton swab.

2. Allow to dry.

3. Reveal your secret message by having your parent heat-treat the paper by placing it in a warm oven, or over a radiator or light bulb.

4. Read your message.

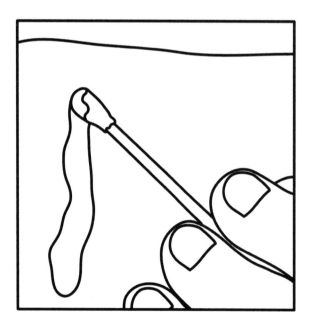

Bases can also be used to make secret messages. However, instead of applying heat to your invisible ink, you will apply an acid solution. When the base combines with the acid, a chemical reaction will occur and your secret message will become visible.

what you will need:

liquid detergent or hand soap

paintbrush or cotton swab

sheet of white paper

purple grape juice

directions:

1. Write your secret message using a base solution with a paintbrush or cotton swab.

2. Allow to dry.

3. Paint over the message with purple grape juice.

4. Read your message.

what you will need:

a chicken

directions:

1. Pick up your chicken and place it lovingly on the ground.

2. Gently place a hand on the chicken's side.

3. Using your other hand, use your pointer finger to draw a line in the dirt starting about two inches from the chicken's beak for about eight inches. Do this ten times.

4. Gently remove your hand from the chicken's side.

5. To everyone's surprise, the chicken will not hop up and run away.

6. Gently pick up the chicken, allow it to eat some corn from your hand, stroke it gently, and place it back into the coop.

! Please be mindful of your pet chicken. Be gentle, and only hypnotize your chicken a few times a year.

A cipher is a fancy name for a secret code. Secret codes have been used in many wars and espionage activities. To the right is an example of the famous cipher used in the Civil War by Elizabeth Van Lew. Elizabeth Van Lew was a southern lady who was a northern spy.

directions:

1. Place a finger on the number running vertically and place another finger on the number that runs horizontally.

2. Where the two fingers meet is the secret coded letter. For example if I want to write a note to a friend to meet me after school by the flag pole my note would look like this:

13 11 11 65 – 13 11 – 66 46 – 65 62 11 – 45 51 53 14 – 41 52 51 11

I would then use my cipher to decode the message:

M E E T - M E - B Y - T H E - F L A G - P O L E

3. Now create your own cipher! Make sure you keep your cipher key in a secret place so that bad guys don't get their hands on it!

6	R	N	B	H	T	X
3	V	1	W	8	4	w
1	E	M	3	J	5	G
5	L	A	9	0	I	D
2	K	7	2	Z	6	S
4	P	O	Y	C	F	q
	1	3	6	2	5	4

WARNING! Always wear thick gloves or use tongs when handling dry ice.

what you will need:

3-gallon container with lid

long-handled spoon

3 cups sugar

18 cups water

3 Tbsp. root beer flavoring

2½ pounds dry ice

directions:

1. Pour sugar, water, and root beer flavoring into container.

2. Stir until sugar is dissolved.

3. Have an adult add the dry ice. Be sure to remind your parents never to touch dry ice with their bare hands because it will blister and burn their skin.

4. Loosely cover the container with the lid and allow root beer to brew for 30-60 minutes before serving.

For a variation, add 1 Tbsp. vanilla extract to the root beer. Other varieties of homemade soda can be made by substituting flavorings. One of my favorites is a combination of cream soda and orange.

Homemade root beer makes a terrific witches' brew for a Halloween party!

This is fun to play as a night game with teenagers!

what you will need:

1 empty can

3 or more family and friends

a large open area surrounded by places to hide such as bushes, trees, buildings, or parked cars.

directions:

1. Place the can in the middle of the open area.

2. Decide where the jail will be.

3. Decide who will be "It."

4. Decide who will be in Jail.

5. "It" closes his eyes and counts to 50 while the other players hide.

6. When "It" has counted to 50, he opens his eyes and begins to look for the other players.

7. Each of the hidden players will come out of hiding when they believe they can

run past "It" and kick the can.

8. If "It" runs and tags a player before they can kick the can, they must go to jail.

9. If the player successfully runs to the can and kicks it without being tagged by "It," everyone in jail is free.

10. The game continues until all players are in jail.

11. If a small child is "It," allow them to call out the players name and hiding place as they place a foot on top of the can.

what you will need:

2 different-looking sets of marbles (at least 5 marbles in a set)

directions:

1. Decide if you will be playing for "keeps" or if you will return the loser's marbles.

2. Choose a player to go first.

3. Draw a circle in the dirt.

4. Each player selects their "shooter" marble.

5. Each player will then scatter an equal number of marbles throughout the circle.

6. Whomever goes first will take their shooter marble and aim at one of their opponent's marbles. Taking careful aim with the shooter marble, they try to knock their opponent's marble out of the circle with their shooter. Be careful not to "fudge" or you will loose your turn. "Fudging" is when the person shooting places their hand inside of the circle.

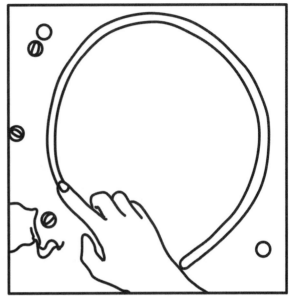

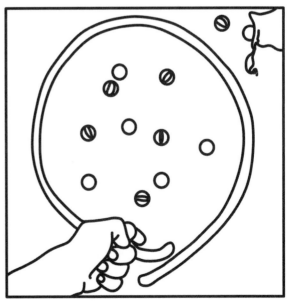

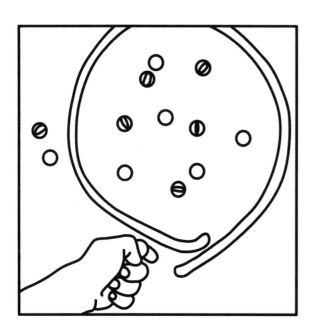

7. If the marble is not knocked out of the circle after the shot, it is the other player's turn.

8. Each player receives a turn until a marble is knocked out of the circle. The player who knocks the marble out of the circle gets another turn and is allowed to keep the marble permanently or until the game is over.

9. The game is over when one opponent's marbles have all been knocked out of the circle.

Raise lady bugs, sea monkeys, triops, frogs from tadpoles, butterflies from caterpillars, or hatch chickens.

When i was a child, i loved when we hatched chickens and ducks, raised rabbits, and fed lambs. Unfortunately, my children did not grow up in the country so what I did was order kits that allowed them to have similar experiences in the city. My children enjoyed raising lady bugs, sea monkeys, triops, frogs from tadpoles, and butterflies from caterpillars.

Below are a few websites where you can purchase these kits:

insectlore.com

butterfly-gifts.com

nature-gifts.com

what you will need:

1 deck of playing cards

enough spoons so that all players but one have a spoon

directions:

The object of the game is to collect 4 cards of one kind. Example: 4 kings, or 4 fives.

1. Place spoons in the middle of the table.

2. Each player is dealt 4 cards by the dealer.

3. The dealer then hands a card, face down, to the person to his right.

4. The person who received the card must choose a card (from their hand) to pass to the person to her right. And so on around the table. At no time may a person have more than 4 cards in their hand.

5. The person before the dealer places their discarded card in a pile to be used when the original pile has been used up.

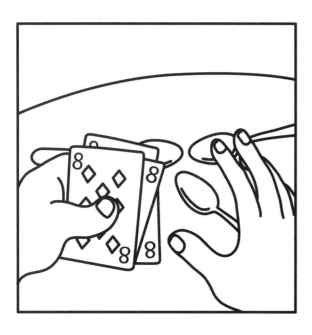

6. The first person who gets 4 of a kind in their hand grabs a spoon.

7. If other players see someone grab a spoon, they must grab a spoon too.

8. The player left without a spoon looses the round. And the game starts over.

9. There should always be 1 less spoon than there are players (like musical chairs), so as players get eliminated, take out spoons accordingly.

10. You may play where each player without a spoon earns letters spelling out the word "S-P-O-O-N-S." When the entire word is spelled out, they are out of the game. OR, you may play where they are eliminated from the game as soon as they do not have a spoon.

what you will need:

PVC straight pipe (24 inches)

2 PVC tees

2 PVC end caps

hacksaw

PVC glue

mini marshmallows

directions:

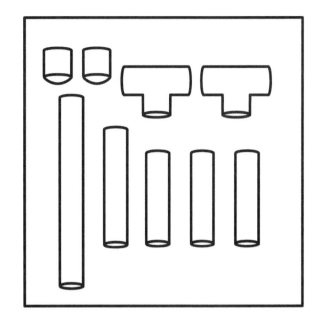

1. First cut the straight pieces with a hacksaw as follows: 7", 5", 4", 4", and 4" long.

2. Glue all the pieces together according to picture.

3. The glue needs at least 2 hours to fully dry. After the glue is dry, your gun is ready!

4. To use, insert a mini marshmallow into the pipe on the mouth piece end (short side).

5. Place your lips around the pipe, aim, and blow with a strong, short burst of

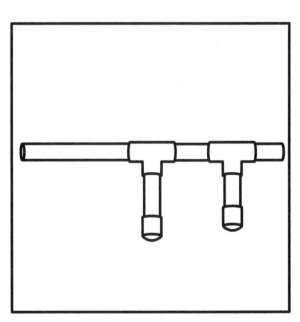

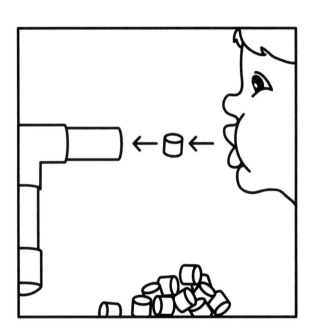

air, emptying your lungs quickly.

!● Never point a gun of any kind at people, animals, or other's property.

what you will need:

candy thermometer

pastry brush

heavy-bottomed pan

wax paper

kitchen shears

¾ cup water

2 cups sugar

1½ cups corn syrup

1 tsp. salt

2 Tbsp. butter, plus enough to butter
fingers

food coloring and flavoring

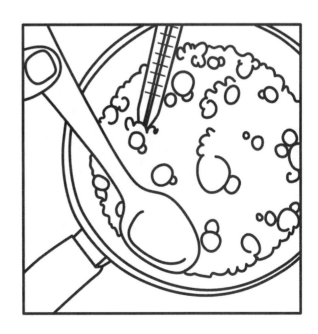

directions:

1. In a heavy-bottomed pan, combine
the water, sugar, corn syrup, and salt.

2. Stir until sugar is dissolved.

3. With a pastry brush, brush insides

of pot to prevent sugar crystals from forming.

4. Heat to 265 degrees, checking temperature with candy thermometer.

5. Gently stir in 2 tablespoons of butter.

6. Allow to cool to the point that it can be handled without burning hands, but still warm to the touch.

7. Add flavoring and food coloring.

8. Butter fingers and begin pulling taffy about 12 inches, folding over and pulling.

9. Stretch taffy until it is too stiff to pull. Roll into a rope and cut with kitchen shears.

10. Wrap pieces in wax paper, twisting ends closed, and store in an airtight container.

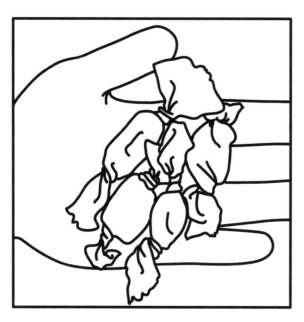

what you will need:

2 2-inch x 2-inch x 8-foot boards

4 $\frac{3}{8}$-inch x 5½-inch lag bolts

4 $\frac{3}{8}$-inch nuts

4 $\frac{3}{8}$-inch lock washers

8 $\frac{3}{8}$-inch flat washers

pencil

measuring tape or ruler

hand saw

safety glasses

drill

$\frac{3}{16}$-inch drill bit

$\frac{13}{32}$-inch drill bit

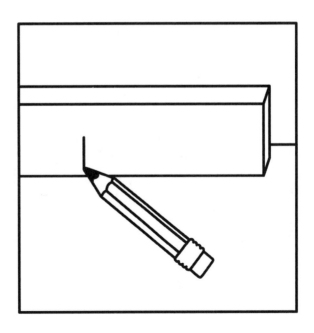

directions:

1. Using measuring tape, measure desired height of foot paddles. We chose 12 inches.

2. Using pencil, mark both pieces of

the wood 12 inches from the bottom.

3. From the top end of the wood, make a mark at 6 inches and another at 12 inches.

4. While wearing safety glasses, cut the wood at the 6-inch and 12-inch marks on both pieces of wood. You should now have four 6-inch pieces of wood and two 7-feet pieces of wood.

5. Measure and mark each of the 6-inch pieces of wood 1½ inches from the end.

6. Measure and mark each of the 7-feet pieces at 1½ inches and 10½ inches from the bottom end.

7. Using a ³⁄₁₆-inch drill bit, drill a pilot hole in the center of each mark. A pilot hole guides the larger bit and also helps prevent the wood from splitting.

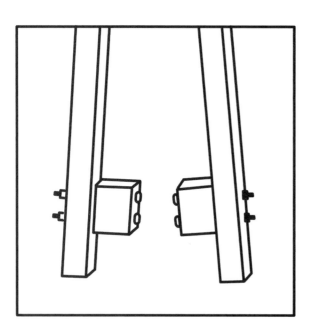

8. Remove the ³⁄₁₆-inch drill bit and replace with the ¹³⁄₃₂-inch drill bit.

9. Re-drill all pilot holes.

10. Place one flat washer on lag bolt.

11. Insert a lag bolt through two of the 6-inch pieces of wood and then through a 7-foot board, followed by a flat washer, a lock washer, and a nut.

12. Repeat bolting process for second hole in 7-foot board.

13. Repeat on second 7-foot board.

❗● As your skill improves you may want to increase the foot paddle height. To do this, simply add more holes up from the original foot paddle in 3-inch intervals.

A whistle can be made from the branch of a tree with soft bark such as Willow, Maple, Aspen, or Cottonwood. It is best to make your whistle in the early summer when the bark is the thickest and also green.

directions:

1. Find a twig that is straight and has a diameter about as thick as an adult thumb (not more than 3/4-inch thick). You need a section about 6-10 inches long with no knots or other twigs growing off it.

2. Next cut your mouth piece at about a 45 degree angle. Then cut across the mouthpiece at the top end at a 90 degree angle to make a shallow and slightly blunt end where your lips go.

3. Now cut the air notch in the top of the bark. The shape, size, and location are fairly important. Don't make the notch too big. About ¼-inch wide should do. Cut just deep enough to mark the wood for later. Cut the part of the notch closest to the mouthpiece by pressing straight down with your knife blade. Then cut the other side of the

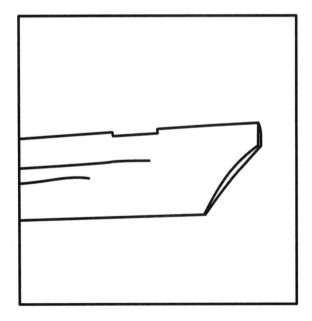

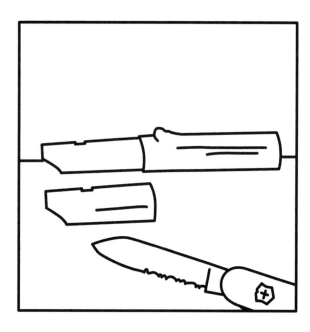

notch with your knife at an angle and going towards the mouth piece and the first cut you made.

4. Next cut a separation ring all the way around the twig, about two-thirds of the way down from the mouthpiece. Cut all the way through the bark and slightly into the wood.

5. Now it is time to slip the bark off the wood on the mouthpiece side. In order to loosen the bark from the stick without damaging the bark, tap on the bark with something blunt like the butt end of your knife. The trick is to tap hard enough to loosen the bark from the wood but not so hard that the bark cracks. Tap up and down on every part of the bark several times, then with a twisting motion try to twist the bark off of the twig. If it does not come off, try tapping more. You can try soaking the twig overnight. If you crack the bark, you will need to start over with a new twig.

6. After removing the bark, it is time to cut out the sound cavity. Find the marks on the wood from where you

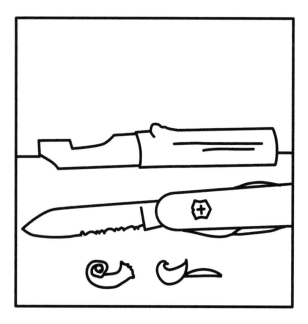

cut the air notch. Cut straight down from the notch side closest to the mouthpiece. Use your knife to hollow out a cavity not more than halfway through the twig. Don't make your cavity so deep that you weaken or break your whistle. The bigger your cavity, the lower the pitch of your whistle will be.

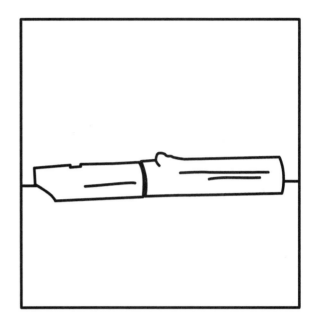

7. Cut a shallow flat sliver off the top edge between the deep cavity and the mouth piece. This will allow the air to be blown from your mouth to the cavity.

8. Next dip your twig into some water and then slip the skin back onto the wood in the exact position it was before you twisted it off.

9. Congratulations! Your whistle is now complete. If it dries out and stops working, you may be able to get it going again by soaking it. Keeping it wrapped in a damp cloth can keep it working longer.

what you will need:

key ring

64 inches of two colors of boondoggle lace

directions:

1. Fold end of one of the pieces of lace so that a loop is formed.

2. Wrap the loop around your index finger.

3. Slip the end of the loop through the middle of the lace that was wrapped around your finger.

4. Slip another piece of lace through the knot opening at the base of the loop.

5. Loosely tighten the knot. Pull the color that was placed through the knot so that it is of equal lengths.

6. Hold the loop facing the floor. Drape the lace down and fold the lace of the same color to form arches. Hold the arches with your fingers.

7. Weave the other color lace over and

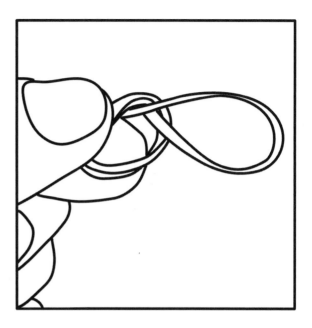

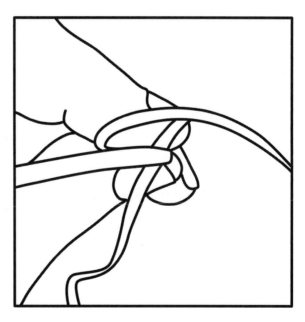

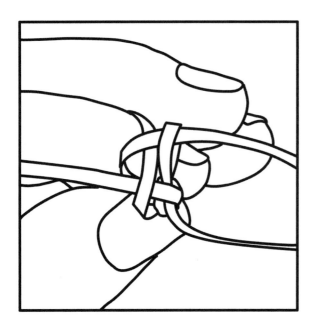

under these arches. Be sure that your lace is not twisted.

8. When your key chain is long enough, tie each of the two colors in a knot.

9. Make another slip knot, sliding the knot close to the last braid. Trim the ends to desired length.

! If you would like to make a spiral pattern, follow steps 1-7 ● and after the first square begin placing the lacing on the diagonal and weave.

Instead of a key chain, you can also make a bracelet following these same steps. You will need the lace 10 times the circumference of your wrist.

As you can see, the only limitation with boondoggling is your imagination! My son, Adam, boondoggled a snake key ring.

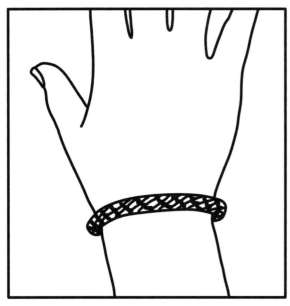

what you will need:

10 jacks

1 bouncy ball

at least two people

directions:

1. Decide who will go first.

2. Toss the jacks out on a hard surface.

3. Begin with "Onesies." Bounce the ball with one hand and while the ball is mid air, scoop up a jack then catch the ball before it bounces again.

4. If you are successful, you are now ready to try for "Twosies." Do the same as before only this time scoop up 2 jacks in your hand before the ball bounces again.

5. Continue until someone reaches "Tensies."

6. It is the next person's turn if the ball bounces a second time, or if the correct number of jacks is not picked up.

7. First person to reach "Tensies" wins.

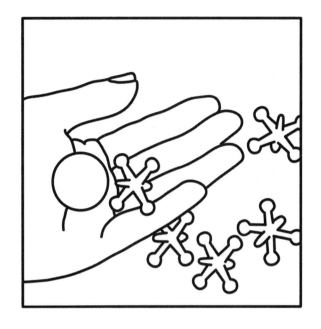

what you will need:

1 glass bottle with an opening at least 1½- 2 inches wide (such as a Snapple® bottle)

½ tsp. rubbing alcohol

1 match

1 hardboiled egg, peeled

directions:

1. Twenty-four hours in advance, wash and dry your bottle (allow it to dry overnight).

2. Hard-boil the egg, allow it to cool, and then peel the shell off.

3. Place ½ teaspoon alcohol in the glass bottle.

4. Have an adult light the match and drop it into the bottle, then immediately place the egg on top of the bottle.

5. Wait a few seconds and the flame will burn up the oxygen in the bottle and create a vacuum. When the vacuum is strong enough, the egg will be sucked

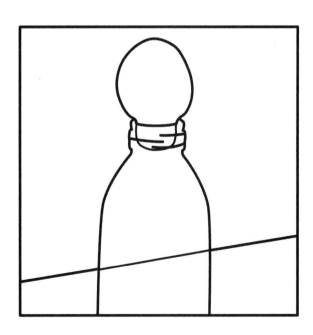

into the bottle. Voila! See if anyone else is able to figure out how you got an egg into the bottle!

This really fun activity was one that my good friend Laura Lee Andersen did with her children.

what you will need:

1 gallon warm water

1 cup dish soap

1 Tbsp. glycerin

1 small plastic kiddie pool

1 hula hoop

1 step stool

directions:

1. One week in advance, mix the warm water, dish soap, and glycerin together between two buckets. Allow the solution to sit out.

2. One week later on a wind-free day or in the garage, have a child sit in the pool on a stool.

3. Pour the solution into the pool.

4. Place the hula hoop in the pool with the child in the middle and then slowly

lift the hula hoop up over child.

5. Have a person take a picture for their scrapbook!

Children may also make giant bubbles by holding the hula hoop up and running around the yard after the hula hoop has been dipped in solution.

Masks can be made from paper bags, gallon bleach or vinegar bottles, casting material, or paper maché. Probably the trickiest part of making a mask is figuring out where to make the holes for the eyes, nose, and mouth for children of different sizes. These instructions are for making a mask from a gallon-size vinegar bottle.

what you will need:

piece of paper

scissors

1 empty plastic gallon-size vinegar bottle, **<u>thoroughly rinsed out</u>**

string

glue

miscellaneous items to decorate mask

directions:

1. Take a piece of paper and place it on the child's face.

2. Gently press the paper around the

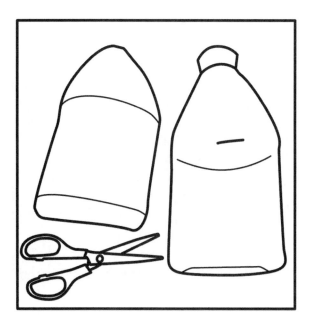

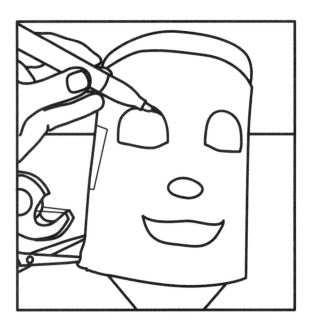

child's features. The indentations in the paper are your pattern.

3. Next cut the shapes of the eyes, nose and mouth out of the paper.

4. Cut the bottom, top, and all but one large side of the plastic vinegar bottle off so you only have the non-handle-side left.

5. Center and tape the paper pattern onto the vinegar bottle.

6. Trace the shapes with a marker.

7. Cut the marked shapes out and remove the pattern.

8. Poke holes on side of mask for tie strings.

9. Thread string through holes and secure with a knot.

10. Decorate the mask with paint, empty paper towel rolls, crepe paper, wrapping paper, feathers, leaves, sand, shells, sequins, pasta, dried beans, construction paper, and anything else a creative mind can think of!

what you will need:

1 large feather

sharp knife or box cutter

bottle of calligraphy ink

paper

directions:

1. Have an adult point the feather and knife away from their body and carefully cut the end of the quill at a 45-degree angle for you.

2. Instruct the adult to carefully carve each side of the quill inward so that the tip is pointed.

3. Dip the quill into the ink.

4. Write a note, dipping quill tip in ink as often as needed. Quill pens are fun for children and adults!

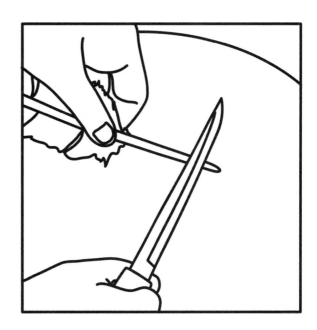

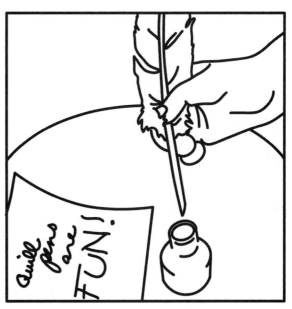

what you will need:

1 10-inch length of semi-flexible clear tubing (⅝-inch diameter)

1 plastic funnel with 5¼-inch diameter mouth and 1¾-inch spout

2 12-foot lengths of surgical tubing (¼-inch outside diameter)

1 18-inch length of nylon rope (⅜-inch diameter)

4 plastic wire ties (zip-ties) for electrical cables

duct tape

heavy-duty scissors or knife

drill

directions:

1. Cut the clear tubing into two 5-inch-long sections to be used for hand holds. If the funnel has a plastic side tab, cut it off.

2. Drill two holes on opposite sides of the funnel; these will be used to thread the tubing through (holes are ¼-inch diameter, placed 1¼-inch apart, and ⅝-inch from the edge.

3. Tie a single knot on one end of the nylon rope. Cut the rope end about ½-inch from the knot. Melt the exposed threads at the cut with a flame to keep the threads from fraying. Pull the rope through the neck of the funnel until the knot catches on the inside of the funnel and the rope extends out the neck of the funnel.

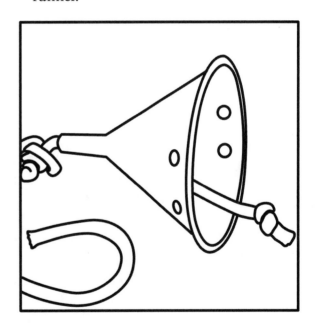

4. Place a mark on the rope 5 inches behind the funnel and tie about four knots in this area for a hand hold. Once again, cut the excess length of rope near the knot and melt the ends of the cut to keep from fraying.

5. Fold one of the 12-inch sections of surgical tubing in half (doubled up section is now 6 inches long) and insert it through the hole in one side of the funnel.

6. Thread the tubing back out the other hole next to it. The mid-section of tubing should be on the inside of the funnel.

7. Slip a piece of clear tubing (hand hold) over the surgical tubing and slide it down and out of the away.

8. Take the two open ends of the tube and tie them around the opposite loop end of the tubing.

9. Now slip the clear tubing (hand hold) back over the new knot. You have now completed one side of the launcher tubing. Repeat steps 5 through 9 for the opposite side of the launcher tubing.

10. Use the wire ties to hold the tubing together at convenient distances. Cover the rope knot on the inside of the launcher with a piece of duct tape to protect the balloon from being punctured by the knot during launch. Your launcher is now complete and should look like the one in the illustration.

11. To use your launcher you will need three people. Two people will stand about 6 feet apart and each will hold one handle. The third person will stretch the funnel backward between the other two by holding onto the rope. Person three will then place the water balloon in the funnel; aim and let go of the rope to launch the balloon.

! Remember to never take aim at people, animals, or the property of others.

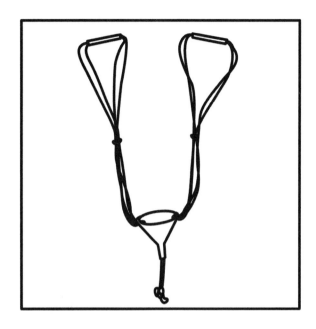

what you will need:

tree branch

1 clothespin

duct tape

pocket knife

rubber bands

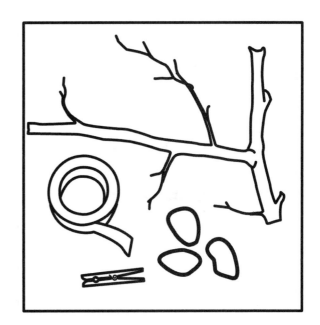

directions:

1. Find a tree branch that has the natural shape of a gun. Remember to get permission before cutting off someone's tree branch. Cut off the branch then trim off all small twigs and bumps until just the hand grip and barrel remain.

2. Once your pistol is formed, secure the clothespin on top of the hand grip using a half-wide strip of duct-tape.

3. Place the clothespin at the back end of the barrel so your thumb can open the clothespin.

4. Cut a shallow notch in the tip of the barrel with a pocket knife. This will help hold the rubber band in place before firing.

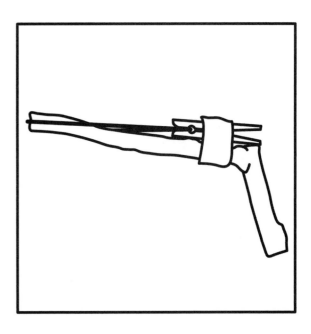

5. Congratulations, your pistol is done! Stretch a rubber band from the tip of the pistol into the mouth of the clothespin. Fire when ready!

! • Never point a gun of any kind at people, animals, or other's property.

what you will need:

1 bicycle tire tube

1 empty plastic 1-liter soda bottle

1 cork the diameter of the opening to
the soda bottle

petroleum jelly

1 drill and bit the size of the bike tire
valve

knife

directions:

1. Cut the bicycle tire tube valve out
of tube, leaving a ring of rubber con-
nected to the valve. Do not throw away
the tube—you can use this to make
other fun projects.

2. Measure and cut the cork if necessary so that when the valve is inserted
through the cork, the threaded portion
of the valve will be visible and the opposite opening will extend into the bottle.

3. Drill a hole in the center of the cork
that is the diameter of the valve.

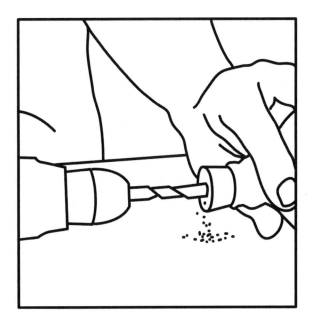

4. Lubricate the valve with the petroleum jelly and slide the valve into the cork.

5. Fill the soda bottle 1/3 full of water.

6. Place the cork into the bottle.

7. Build a launch pad.

8. Find an open field and place the rocket on the launch pad.

9. Attach the bicycle pump to the rocket and begin pumping. When enough pressure has built up the rocket will blast off!

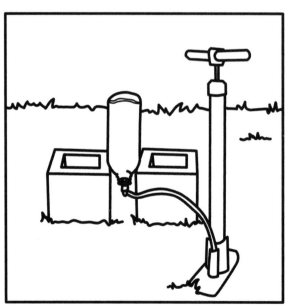

what you will need:

1 jar or bottle with a lid

water

baby oil or vegetable oil (the clearer the color, the better)

food coloring

directions:

1. Fill jar ⅓ full of water.

2. Add enough food coloring to color the water. The darker the color, the better.

3. Swirl jar so water is evenly colored.

4. Fill jar to the top with the oil.

5. Tightly screw lid on jar.

6. Slowly tilt the jar back and forth. Watch what happens

7. Rock the jar slowly, then faster. Watch what happens.

8. Shake the jar and set it on the counter, then watch what happens.

Pirate Treasure Hunt

Every year before the start of school, I would hold a pirate treasure hunt for my children. It was a wonderful activity that we all looked forward too. The children would dress up in pirate clothes from Halloween, complete with eye patches, gold clip on earrings, bandanas over their heads, ragged shorts, and red-and-white-striped shirts. One year my daughter Rachel even placed our cockatiel, King Boaz, on her shoulder.

I would hide treasure clues in the house that would lead the children all over the neighborhood. Eventually the children would find the treasure map which would lead them to the pirate booty!

Our pirate booty would consist of candy, ice cream coupons, movie tickets, and small trinkets.

Staying up Late and Getting French Fries

It was midnight (i had allowed the children to stay up past their nine p.m. bedtime) and I had just finished painting the hallway leading to our bedrooms. I told the children that it was time for bed but there was one more thing we needed to do. The children assumed it was scripture study and groaned and stated that they were too tired. I then told them they were wrong. It wasn't scripture time, it was French fry time. Both of my children's eyes nearly popped out of their eye sockets before they began dancing and whooping! I coyly added before we headed to the car, "Maybe we shouldn't go if you are so tired?" Naturally they smiled and emphatically sang out, "Oh no Mom. We aren't tired. We feel great!"

Now my son is a young man, but if we are driving home from a late-night activity and pass a Wendy's, he will often bring up the time we stayed up past bedtime and bought fries.

Dancing in the Rain

One year we were living in Arizona during the monsoon season. Our gutters were full from all of the rain. Rachel and I put on our swimsuits and played in the rain, splashing in the gutters. As we danced in the rain the neighbors would briskly close their blinds and curtains because their children wanted to come out and play too! Rachel laughed and played all the more. This memory is one Rachel continues to reminisce about. Funny how it is one of her favorite memories and it didn't cost a thing besides my time.

Eat Dessert First

My daughter liked eating home lunch at school. One morning I decided to give Rachel a treat. Little did I know that this simple act would be a lasting memory for her. What I did was pack her sandwich on the bottom of her lunch box and covered it with a cloth. Next

I put in an ice pack, followed by an ice cream sandwich and then another ice pack. The last item I put in her lunch box was a note that said, "Eat your dessert first! Love, Mom." All of the children at her lunch table couldn't believe that Rachel had an ice cream sandwich in her lunch box, and they found it even more unbelievable that her mom said to eat dessert first!

Why do i mention these simple experiences? Because my children do not particularly recall our elaborate and expensive yearly vacations unless we are looking at scrapbooks. Instead, they fondly reminisce about inexpensive activities such as pirate treasure hunts, splashing in gutters, and eating fries past their bedtime. I have learned that expensive activities do not necessarily equate to cherished memories. No, sharing of ones time doing inexpensive, out of the ordinary activities create lasting childhood memories!

what you will need:

2 cups white glue

1½ cups water plus ⅓ cup

2 tsp. borax soap

directions:

1. Stir together the glue and 1½ cups water

2. In another bowl, stir together ⅓ cup water and the borax soap.

3. Combine the contents of the two bowls, stirring until the glue mixture sets up. This is "Glurch."

4. Remove the set up portion from the bowl and mix in more of the water and borax solution as needed until all of the glue mixture has turned into "Glurch."

5. Enjoy playing with this squishy putty! Kids love to play with it because of its odd texture.

what you will need:

1 cup white flour

¼ cup salt

2 Tbsp. cream of tartar

1 cup water

1 Tbsp. oil

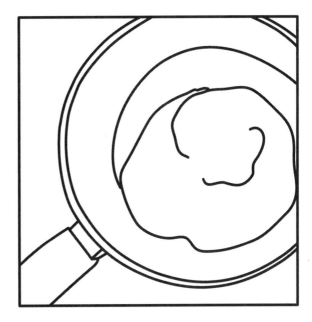

directions:

1. Mix all ingredients in a medium pan over medium heat for 3-5 minutes, or until mixture forms a ball in the pan.

2. Remove from pan and knead dough on a lightly floured counter. Store dough in an airtight container.

! We have used salt dough to make homemade Christmas ornaments. ● We insert a small paper clip into the top of the shape for the hook holder and then let them dry out so they are hard. It's a lot of fun to see what shapes the kids make and to talk about them each year when the tree is decorated.

These cookies were and still are my children's favorite cookies to make and to eat!

what you will need:

- ⅔ cup butter
- 1 cup sugar
- 2 tsp. vanilla extract
- 2 eggs
- 2½ cups flour
- ½ cup cocoa
- ½ tsp. baking powder
- ¼ tsp. salt

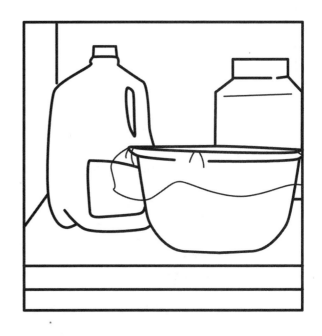

directions:

1. In a large bowl, cream butter, sugar, and vanilla until light and fluffy.

2. Add eggs, blending well.

3. Combine dry ingredients and blend into the creamed mixture.

4. Chill until dough is firm enough to handle.

5. Heat oven to 350°.

6. Shape dough into animal shapes.

7. Bake until set; time varies depending on size of animal shape. Typically 8-10 minutes for a small 2-inch animal shape.

what you will need:

1 quart half and half

2 cups milk

sugar to taste (1-2 cups)

1 Tbsp. vanilla extract

2 cups fresh fruit, chopped

ice cream maker or freezer

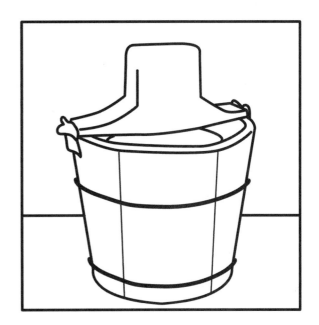

directions:

1. Combine all ingredients except fruit in a large bowl.

2. Stir until sugar is dissolved.

3. Add chopped fruit.

4. Place batter in ice cream canister.

5. Layer ice and rock salt, finishing with rock salt around the ice cream canister.

If you do not have an ice cream maker, you can still make ice cream in the freezer. Place the ice cream batter in a large rectangular cake pan and every few hours stir the batter. Serve when ice cream is frozen to desired consistency.

what you will need:

1 (14 oz.) bag caramels

2 Tbsp. water

5 popsicle sticks

5 apples, refrigerated

1 cookie sheet

wax paper

butter

directions:

1. Cover cookie sheet with wax paper.

2. Generously butter wax paper.

3. Wash, thoroughly dry, and remove stems from apples. Push popsicle stick into top of apple, where stem grows.

4. Return apples to refrigerator. Cold apples are the secret to fabulous caramel apples.

5. Unwrap caramels and place in a small pot.

6. Add water and place lid on pot.

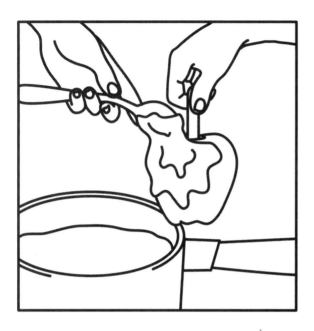

Cook on medium heat, stirring frequently.

7. When caramels are melted and smooth, usually 3-5 minutes, remove pot from burner.

8. Holding apple by popsicle stick and, over the pot, spoon melted caramel over the apple.

9. When apple is coated, repeat.

10. Scrape off excess caramel from bottom of apple. You may chose to roll the apple in candies, cookie crumbs, nuts, sprinkles at this time.

11. Place apple on buttered wax paper and repeat with other apples.

12. Once all apples are coated in caramel, place cookie sheet with apples on it in the refrigerator for 1 hour, and then serve.

When your children are older they may want to make caramel apples from scratch. Try the following delicious recipe.

what you will need:

1 cup butter

2 cups brown sugar

1 cup light corn syrup

1 can sweetened condensed milk

2 tsp. vanilla

8-10 popsicle sticks

8-10 apples

candy thermometer

directions:

1. Combine all ingredients except vanilla in pot.

2. Cook over medium heat, stirring constantly, until caramel reaches 248°.

3. Remove from heat and add vanilla.

4. Spoon caramel over apples.

5. Place on buttered wax paper and refrigerate for 1 hour before serving.

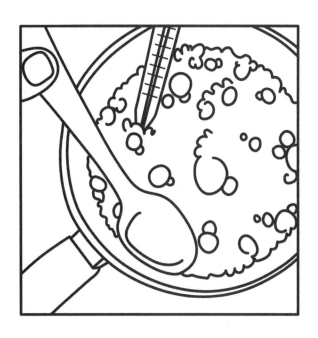

what you will need:

2 lbs. eye of round sliced to 1/8th-inch thickness

½ cup soy sauce

½ cup Worcestershire sauce

1 tsp. liquid smoke

1 Tbsp. red wine vinegar

4 Tbsp. brown sugar

1 tsp. garlic powder (NOT garlic *salt*)

1½ tsp. onion powder (NOT onion *salt*)

1¼ tsp. ground black pepper

1/8 tsp. cayenne pepper

dehydrator or oven

directions:

1. Trim meat completely of fat.

2. Blend all ingredients except meat in a bowl. Then add meat, one piece at a time.

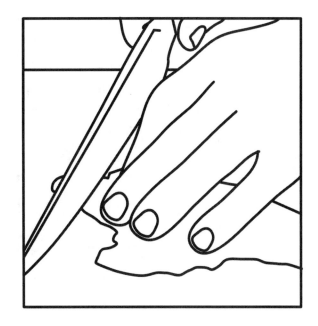

3. Cover with plastic wrap and marinate overnight in the refrigerator

4. The next day, remove meat from bowl and place on drying racks of dehydrator, being careful that meat strips do not overlap.

5. Dehydrate for 8-10 hours, or until jerky is dried to the point that it does not break in two when bent.

6. Store in plastic bags or covered containers.

If you don't have a dehydrator you can still make jerky:

Place some foil on the bottom rack of your oven.

On the top rack of the oven, place meat strips on a wire cooling rack.

Leave the oven door cracked open and bake at 130°-150° until jerky is dried to the point that it will crack but not break in two when bent.

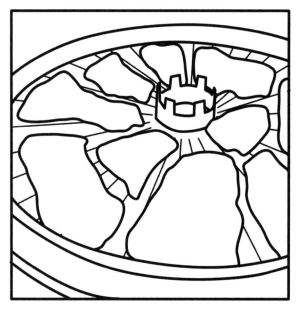

what you will need:

1 cup water

food coloring

3 cups sugar

mason jar

wooden skewer, or piece of thick, rough string

directions:

1. In a small sauce pan, bring the water to a rolling boil.

2. Stir in sugar and food coloring until dissolved.

3. Pour sugar solution into a mason jar.

4. Suspend the wooden skewer or string in the solution so that it doesn't touch the bottom of the jar.

5. Wait and wait and wait. DO NOT pick up or move the jar for several days. Over time, the water will evaporate and the sugar crystals will attach to the skewer. As more time passes, the sugar crystals will cover the skewer and grow larger.

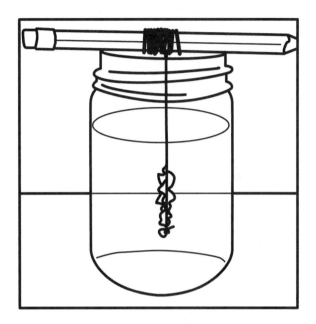

When i was a young person, this was one of my favorite activities. We would have playoffs and afterward have a BBQ. It was great fun!

what you will need:

2 blocks of ice

1 hill

family and friends

directions:

1. You and another person determine the starting line at the top of the hill and the finish line at the bottom of the hill.

2. Each racer sits down on their block of ice and when "Go" is yelled, each racer lifts their legs as they race on their block of ice down the hill.

3. The first one who reaches the finish line wins the race.

We used to have slumber parties almost every weekend during the summer. They were so much fun. We would play games, eat lots of junk food, and laugh and talk into the night. One fun activity we did was gather in a closet, turn out the lights, and look for sparks as one of us chewed Wint-O- Green Lifesavers®. It's so much fun to see sparks when someone eats.

what you will need:

1 package Wint-O-Green Lifesavers®

family and friends

1 dark closet

directions:

1. Go into a closet

2. Place the Lifesaver in your mouth and position it between your molars and turn off the light.

3. Bite down quick and hard keeping your mouth open so that the Lifesaver is visible. Others will see bright blue sparks when you bite down!

Another fun activity we used to do at slumber parties was levitate someone. You really don't levitate them, but it's fun just the same.

what you will need:

several people

directions:

1. Have a person lie on their back on the floor.

2. All of the remaining people gather equally around the person on the floor, placing their hands under the person's body.

3. On the count of three, everyone attempt to lift the person. It will be awkward and nearly impossible.

4. Now, tell the person on the floor to concentrate on the words that will be chanted.

5. Teach the words: "Light as a feather. Stiff as a board."

6. Have everyone chant this phrase three times with equal loudness.

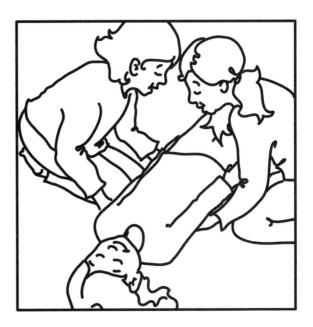

7. Say the phrase again, only louder, and have the others follow suit, chanting it three times.

8. This is repeated about 10 times; each time increasing the volume but never yelling.

9. On the 10th time, the people lift the person up as before, only this time they are "Light as a feather" and "Stiff as a board!"

what you will need:

1⅔ yards of fleece (8 inches wide)

scissors

! Be sure to choose a fleece pattern that looks the same on both sides. ● Sometimes one side of fleece is duller in color.

directions:

1. Place fabric on a hard cutting surface.

2. To make the fringe, cut each end of the scarf in ½-inch sections, about 5 inches in length. To make things easier for the children, I place masking tape 5 inches from the end of the fabric as a marker for cutting depth.

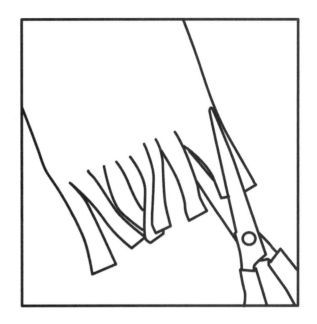

One mother's day i walked into my bedroom and found this sweet pillow on my side of the bed. I turned around and there was my son, Adam (age 7) beaming up at me from the doorway. Nine years later, every time I snuggle up to this pillow, I see his little face glowing with pride!

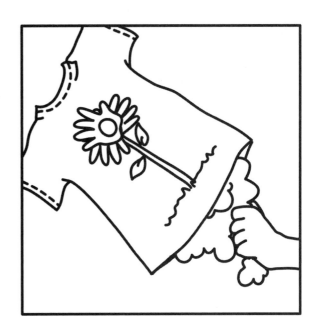

what you will need:

1 T-shirt

polyfiber fill

sewing machine

directions:

1. Stitch the sleeves and neck of the T-shirt closed.

2. Fill the T-shirt with poly-fiber fill.

3. Stitch the bottom closed.

4. Fringe the bottom of the pillow by making cuts through the fabric, every $1/2$ inch, approximately four inches in, being careful not to cut stitching.

what you will need:

yarn (Begin with a thicker yarn for small children, and then go as thin as you like with practice.)

crochet hook (I used a size F, but first-timers will do better with a larger size.)

24 beads

hair elastic

scissors

directions:

1. First, thread 24 beads onto yarn. Slide the beads away from the end of the yarn.

2. Hold yarn stretched between fingers and thumb.

3. Make a slip-knot around the crochet hook with the yarn. Loop the yarn as seen in the illustration. Slip one loop through the other and pull. Insert the crochet hook in the loop.

4. Hold the elastic in your left hand.

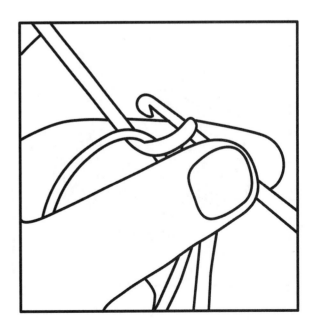

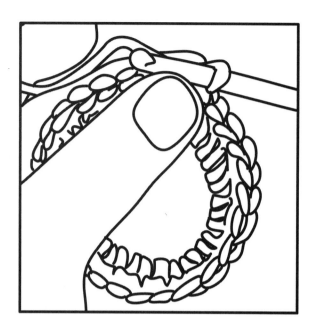

Thread the elastic over the crochet hook and yarn. Using the crochet hook, reach over the elastic and hook the yarn and bring it through the loop on the hook. You have just made your first chain stitch! Continue chain stitching around the elastic. It will take 24 stitches to circle the elastic.

5. Continue around the elastic a second time, only this time, place the crochet hook under one section of the row you just created. Continue around the row.

6. It is now time to add a bead! Make two chain stitches. Slide a bead down to the end of the two chain stitches. Make a stitch over the bead. Just pretend the bead isn't even there.

7. Make one chain stitch toward the elastic. Repeat the process, adding all 24 beads.

8. After all beads have been added, tie off your stitch and enjoy your new hair elastic.

what you will need:

3 canning rings

spool of jute

white glue

directions:

1. Paint a canning ring with glue.

2. Wrap the canning ring with jute.

3. Glue end of jute to the side of the canning ring.

4. Repeat steps 1-3 with remaining canning rings.

5. Fasten the jute-covered canning rings together with jute. I use a simple square knot.

You can also make a place mat or a jute canning ring doormat. Decide what shape and how large you would like your place mat or doormat to be. Follow the steps for the hot pad, but just use more jute-covered canning rings.

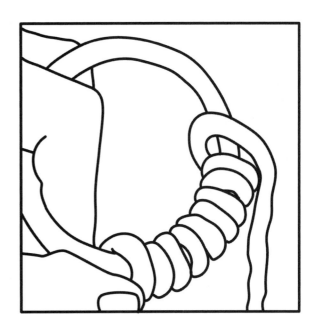

what you will need:

key ring

2 24-inch pieces of jute, or any medium thickness string or yarn

scissors

ruler

directions:

1. Find the middle of the pieces of jute by placing the two ends together and running fingers up to where the loop is.

2. Place the loop inside of the key ring.

3. Slip the double pieces of jute through the loop, making sure that the key ring is in the middle of the knot.

4. Tie a knot as close to the key ring as possible.

5. Do the same with the other piece of jute.

6. Decide how far you would like your knots to be. I do every inch. Tie a knot in each of the four strings, making sure

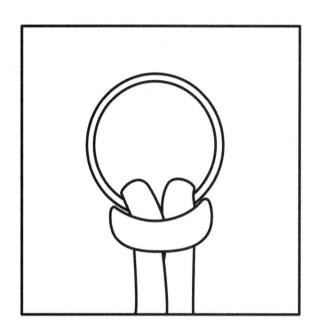

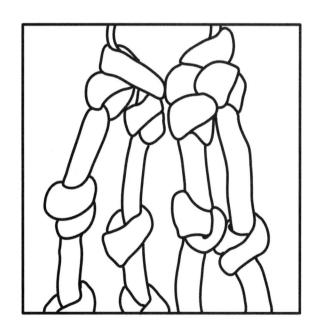

that the knots are tight.

7. When you would like to finish your key chain, tie one knot using all four strings.

If you would like a fancy key chain, slip a bead on before tying the knot. Once the bead is in place, tie a knot to hold it in place. Continue adding bead on each string as desired.

Another fun idea using jute: A jute fashion belt can be made by using a belt ring and about 4-5 times the child's waist circumference of jute for each string.

what you will need:

cardboard

1 roll of jute

scissors

ruler

darning needle (Be sure it is large enough for jute to be threaded through the eye of the needle.)

directions:

1. Decide what size you would like your mat to be.

2. Cut one-inch-deep "Vs", one inch apart, for a 13 x 18-inch piece of cardboard.

3. Wrap jute down width and around the back of the cardboard notch on the other end.

4. Take a long piece of jute and begin weaving the jute to the right, over the first piece of wrapped jute, followed by going under the next piece of jute, alternating this pattern until you reach

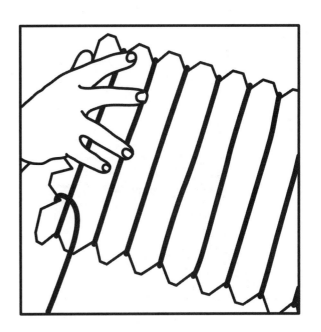

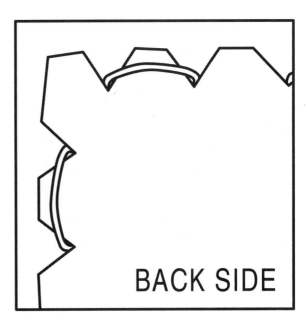

BACK SIDE

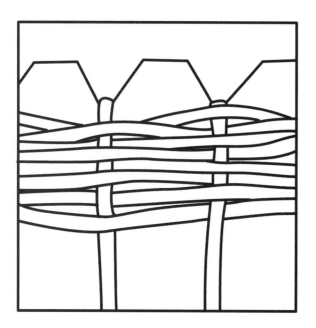

the opposite side of the cardboard. Reverse the pattern and weave toward the left. Be sure to pull the jute evenly and push each weaved row snuggly to the top. When you need more jute, cut another long piece and tie it to the end. Don't worry about the ends; just tuck them into your mat.

5. When you reach the end of your width of cardboard, tuck the ends in and slip the yarn off of the cardboard.

Okay—so you don't really pick them up by their ears—it just looks that way.

directions:

1. Take your child and lightly place your fingers on their ears so it looks like you are pinching them.

2. Instruct the child to stiffen their arms and pull down on your forearms as hard as they can, as you lift them off of the ground.

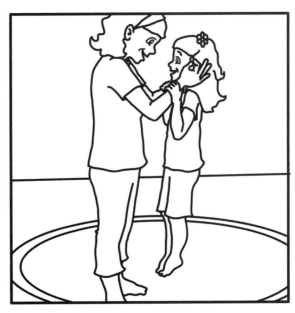

directions:

1. Have a child sit down on a chair and place their hand, palm down, on the top of their head.

2. Have an obviously stronger person grasp the child's forearm from behind and attempt to pull the hand up from their head.

3. Participants, as well as audience members, will be surprised when he can't lift her hand from her head. Be prepared for everyone to want to try to lift her hand from her head.

directions:

1. Instruct a child to stand close to a wall.

2. Have the child stiffen their arm.

3. Instruct the child to press the back side of their hand into the wall as hard as they can, applying even pressure for one minute, longer if the person is muscular.

4. Have the child move away from the wall and relax their arm completely. Their arm will float up!

directions:

1. Have a person stronger than yourself bend his arms and place their elbows firmly into their sides.

2. Next, have him make a fist with each hand, rotating his wrist inward, toward the center of his body.

3. Have him place one fist on top of the other.

! For the trick to work, it is essential that his elbows are in, and his fists are turned inward at the wrists and tightly clenched!

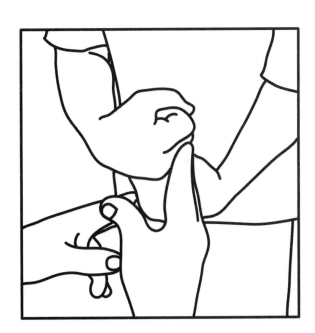

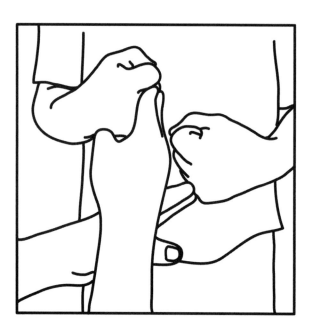

4. Now take two fingers, and in one quick motion, knock their fists from off of each other. No matter how hard he tries to keep his fists on top of each other, he won't be able to. It's magic!

what you will need:

1¾ yard fleece

scissors

directions:

1. Cut 5-inch x 5-inch squares off from each corner of fleece.

2. Make 1-inch wide and 5-inch deep cuts around fabric. (I use masking tape for an easy marker for depth of cuts.)

3. Tie a knot at the base of each strip.

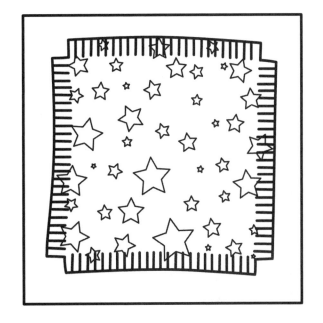

There are many designs and propellants for potato cannons. If you are interested in making a potato cannon, investigate what is legal/illegal for your community and search for websites with appropriate instructions.

! Warning: Potato cannons are dangerous! They are also considered weapons or firearms and are illegal in some states and countries. Be informed and be law-abiding!

I made what seemed to be hundreds of these for a Daddy Daughter Dance. Our theme for the evening was "Paper Roses." I still remember dancing with my daddy to the song, "Paper Roses," sung by Marie Osmond.

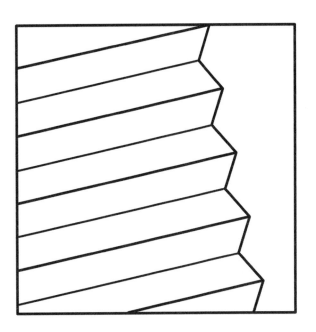

what you will need:

4 6-inch x 12-inch pieces of tissue paper

1 green pipe cleaner

scissors

ruler

directions:

1. Place all 4 pieces of tissue paper on top of each other. Using a 1-inch fold, fan-fold the tissue paper.

2. Twist the pipe cleaner in the middle of the folded tissue paper.

3. Using scissors, round the ends of the tissue paper.

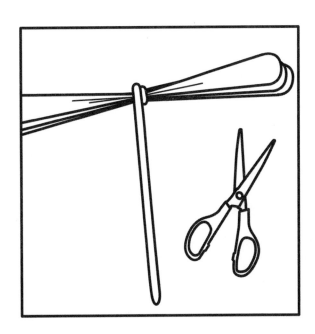

4. Gently pull a layer of tissue paper upward. Continue until all layers have been separated.

! This is a messy project; wear old clothes and remember to cover your working area with newspapers for easy cleanup.

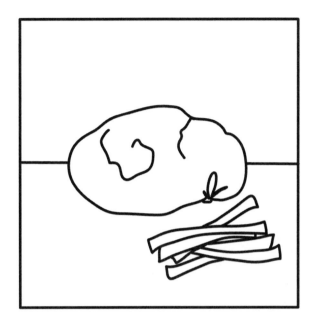

what you will need:

1 cup water

½ cup flour

1 Tbsp. salt

newspaper for stuffing

torn strips of newspaper

plastic bags

masking tape

· paint

directions:

1. In a large bowl, combine water, flour, and salt.

2. Stir until well mixed.

3. Cover your working area with newspaper.

4. Decide on your project's shape and

fill the plastic bag with newspaper accordingly. Tie off the bottom of the bag.

5. Take torn strips of newspaper and dip in paper maché paste.

6. Remove excess paste by gently running your fingers down the strip.

7. Drape strips over plastic bag shape(s).

8. Allow dry. Typically within a day, your project will be dry. The way to tell if it is dry is by touching the paper maché; if it is cold to the touch it is still wet.

9. If using multiple different plastic bag pieces, use masking tape to tape the pieces together to form your shape.

10. Cover masking tape with strips of newspaper dipped in paper maché paste and allow to dry. When paper maché is completely dry, paint project.

O ne year when my children were in elementary school, they wanted to make home-made Christmas gifts for their grandparents. The children decided that their grandparents needed rice bag heating pads because of their aching joints.

what you will need:

1/3-yard flannel fabric (Look in the remnant section. I typically pay under a dollar for 1/3-yard of fabric.)

rice

straight pins

sewing machine

thread

sewing needle

directions:

1. Cut 2 identical pieces of fabric into desired length and shape. We usually make two or three rice bag heating pads from 1/3 of a yard of fabric.

2. Pin the 2 pieces of fabric together, inside out.

3. Sew ½ inch from the edge of the fabric, along all the sides but leaving a 3-inch section unsewn.

4. Carefully turn the fabric inside out through the unsewn section.

5. Fill with rice.

6. Turn the edges of the unsewn section inside and hand stitch close.

7. Make a gift note with warming instructions. Typically 3-4 minutes in a microwave will sufficiently warm the rice.

I can't even count the number of candles I made as a kid. This was such a fun activity because I could use the candles I made for gifts, which brought a sense of personal satisfaction!

what you will need:

1 cardboard milk carton

1 tapered candle

wax

wax coloring (I used old crayons that were too short to color with. I chopped them up and mixed them into the wax. Be creative; try the same color scheme or a rainbow of colors.)

ice cubes

old cooking pot

stove

directions:

1. Clean and dry a cardboard milk carton.

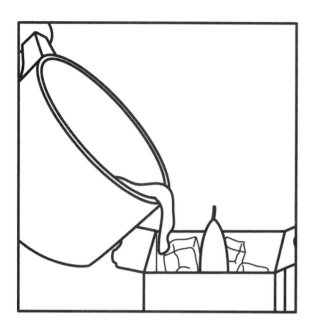

2. In an old pot, melt wax over medium heat. Once wax has melted, add coloring.

3. Insert tapered candle and hold in place as you fill the milk carton with ice cubes. Remove your hands; the ice will hold the candle in place.

4. Have an adult carefully pour melted wax into milk carton. Do not move the milk carton. Allow your candle to cool for two days.

5. After two days, your candle will be solid. Drain off the water from the melted ice cubes. Carefully tear off the milk carton. Enjoy the fun shape of your candle.

! Candles need to cure for at least two weeks before they are ● burned or they will melt away.

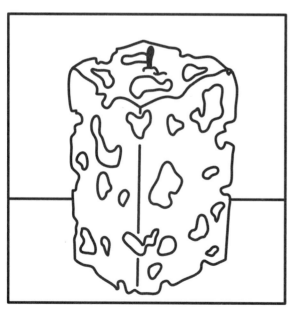

One rainy day i had nothing to do so I made up a fun game. My brother and I played "washer toss" many times when we couldn't play outdoors.

what you will need:

1 washer about the weight of a quarter for each player.

markers

an uncarpeted floor

piece of rope or string or building blocks

a wall

directions:

The rules of the game: You may not cross the line with your body. The closest washer to the base-board wins that toss. Best 5 out of 10 tosses wins the game.

1. Decorate your washer with the marker and allow to it dry.

2. Mark off on the floor, using, rope, string, or building blocks, an agreed

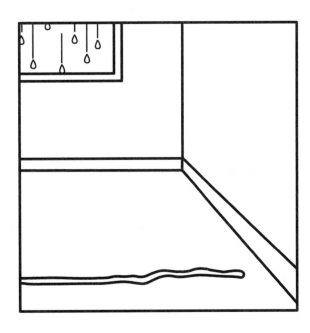

upon distance from the wall.

3. Each player tosses their washer, being careful not to cross over the line. The player whose washer is closest to the wall's base-board wins the tossing match. The first player to win 5 tosses wins the game!

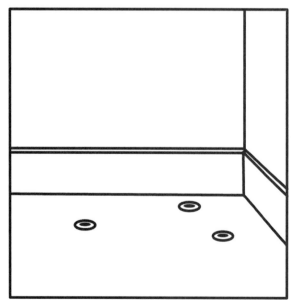

what you will need:

cloth (or old, large T-shirts) cut into
10 strips, ½-inch wide by 16-inch
long (If you use old T-shirts, just
cut the sleeves into ½-inch wide
strips and you won't need to sew.)

additional cloth (or T-shirts) cut into
½-inch strips

scissors

1 large circular embroidery hoop

sewing machine

directions:

1. Bring a strip of cloth together,
forming a loop, and sew the loose ends
together.

2. Repeat for all 10 strips.

3. Stretch the 10 loops of fabric over
hoop.

4. Evenly space the loops of fabric
around the hoop so that it looks like
bicycle wheel spokes.

5. In the center of the "wheel," tie one

of the strips to a "Spoke."

6. Begin weaving a strip of cloth over one "spoke" and then under the next "spoke;" continue over one "spoke" then under the next.

7. Tie more fabric to the strip as needed.

8. Once you have weaved up to 1 inch from the hoop, tie the strip to a "spoke."

9. Cut each of the loops one at a time, tying knots as you go around the hoop cutting the loops.

Now that you have the idea, you can make any size hot pad or rug you want. For instance, if you would like to make a square rug, take a piece of wood the size of the rug you would like to make and hammer nails around the edge. Nails should be spaced every ½ inch for a hot pad and every 5-6 inches for a large throw rug. Remember to sew your strips of fabric so that they will fit snuggly when stretched across the nails. You could also make a rug using a hula hoop, or pot holders from different-sized embroidery hoops.

When i was in elementary school my mother decided we would have a homemade Christmas; this meant even our wrapping paper had to be homemade. I wrapped presents in the newspaper comics. I wrapped presents in brown paper and used rustic decorations, and then I tried making crayon tissue paper. It turned out great! Thirty-five years later I decided to have a homemade Christmas with my children. They loved making the wrapping paper!

what you will need:

old crayons

handheld pencil sharpener

tissue paper

iron and ironing board

paper grocery bag

directions:

1. Cut out the bottom of the grocery bag. You should have a piece of brown grocery bag paper.

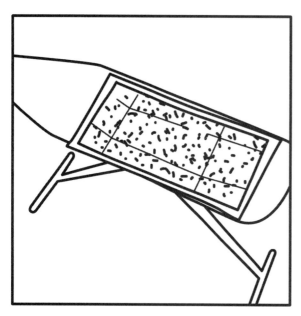

2. Place grocery bag paper on ironing board. This is to protect your ironing board pad from the crayon wax.

3. Place one sheet of tissue paper on top of grocery bag paper.

4. Take old crayons and sharpen the old crayons over the tissue paper so the shavings fall on it.

5. Sandwich the crayon shavings by placing another sheet of tissue paper over the first.

6. Gently press a warm iron on the tissue paper. It will not take long for the wax to melt. Press iron down; do not rub, as crayon wax will smear when heated.

7. Remove the tissue paper from ironing board and allow to cool.

8. Clean off wax from bottom of iron.

9. Wrap present.

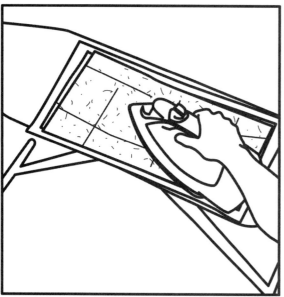

In the fifth or sixth grade, our art teacher gave us an assignment to collect trash from the road and make something from it. I made a really cool picture frame. My mom gave me an old picture frame and I glued my "art" trash onto the frame. Once the glue dried, I spray painted the frame metallic gold.

For my children, we didn't decorate picture frames with trash, but we did collect memories by making theme picture frames from vacations, for instance, shells and drift wood from a vacation at the ocean. We have also made seasonal picture frames using dried flowers gathered at family picnics, brilliantly colored autumn leaves and acorns for fall, and homemade salt dough snowmen and Christmas trees for winter picture frames. Picture frames decorated with assorted dried beans and pasta are always easy and fun to create as well.

Another fun idea for children is to suggest that they make a picture frame that describes how they

see themselves. Perhaps they will select favorite miniature toys such as army men, baseball cards, crayons, candy wrappers, beads, or marbles to glue on their frame. Be sure to have construction paper, glitter, stickers, and of course pictures of each child, to place in their homemade, personalized frame.

what you will need:

1 large button with 2 holes

1 yard embroidery floss

directions:

1. Thread the embroidery floss through the holes in the button.

2. Tie the ends of the floss together. Move the button so that it is in the middle of the floss.

3. Place one finger through each end of the floss loop.

4. Holding one finger still and keeping the floss taut, wind the floss up by twirling your other finger while it is inside the looped floss.

5. Once finished winding your hummer, slowly stretch out the floss; this motion will unwind the floss. Before the floss unwinds completely, bring the floss ends slowly together to rewind the floss.

6. Continue the in-and-out motion of your hands. Soon your speed will increase and the button will be humming!

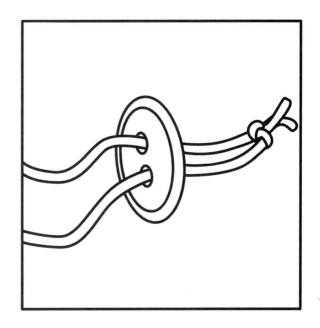

Growing up we would often go camping at the ocean. My dad would take us out at low-tide and we would collect shells and drift wood. Once home, we would make wind chimes out of the items we had collected. We have also made wind chimes out of metal tubes, pieces of bamboo, and just about anything that clangs when hit together by a breeze.

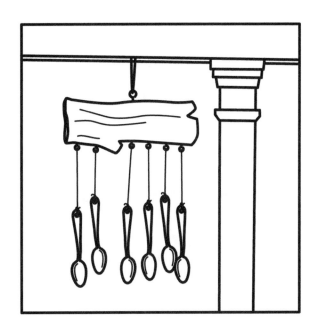

what you will need:

a piece of wire or chain

1 large eye screw

a piece of wood (wood may be sanded and varnished/painted if desired)

small eye screws

fishing line cut into various lengths

items of interest that make noise when hit together by a breeze

directions:

1. Find the center, on the top side, of the wood.

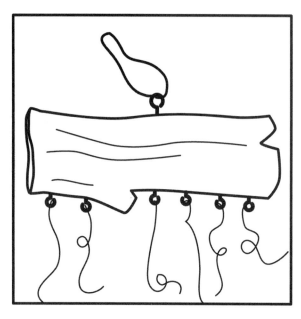

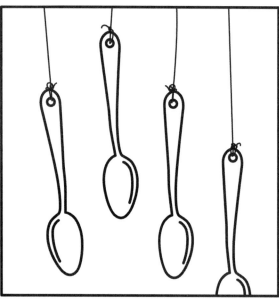

2. At the center point, screw in a large eye screw.

3. Loop the wire or chain through the eye screw. This will be used to hang your wind chime.

4. Screw small eye screws into the bottom of the wood.

5. Tie fishing line through eye screws.

6. Tie items onto the other end of the fishing line, making sure that they will clang when blown by a breeze. You may need to have a parent drill holes through the objects so that they can be securely tied onto the fishing line.

7. Hang your wind chimes from your porch and wait for your wind chime and a gentle breeze to make beautiful music together.

what you will need:

2 7-inch by 3½-inch by ½-inch pieces
  of wood

4 5-inch pieces of ¼ inch satin ribbon
  (2 of one color and 2 of a second
  color)

8 flat head thumb tacks

1 dollar bill

measuring tape

pencil

sand paper and stain, if desired

directions:

1. If desired, sand and stain blocks of
wood.

2. Place blocks side-by-side.

3. Draw a mark with a pencil 1¾ inch
from the top and bottom of block #1 on
the outer or left side and on the inner
side or left side of block #2.

4. Draw a mark with a pencil 2½
inches down from the top and bottom of

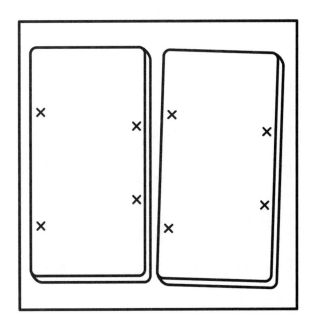

the inside or right-hand-side of block #1.

5. Draw a mark with a pencil 2½ inches down from the top and bottom of the outer or right-hand-side of block #2.

6. Fasten one end of the one color of ribbon with a thumb tack where the 1¾-inch mark was made at the top of block #1.

7. Repeat with other color ribbon for the bottom 1¾-inch mark on block #1. This is the back surface of your magic blocks.

8. Pull the ribbon around to the front side of the block and attach it to the back surface of the second block with a thumb tack at the 1¾-inch mark from the top. The second block is positioned right next to block #1.

9. Repeat with second other color ribbon for the bottom of the block.

10. Use thumb tacks to fasten the first color ribbons on the second block at the 2½-inch marks.

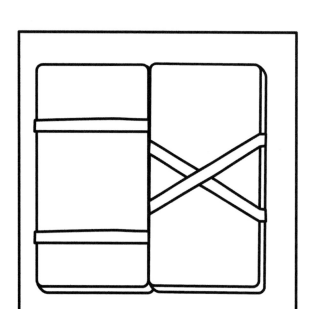

11. Cross the ribbons so that they make an "X" on the front side of the block.

12. Use thumb tacks to attach the first color ribbons to the back side of the first block at the 2½-inch marks.

13. Insert a dollar bill between the ribbons on the block of your choice.

14. Close the block.

15. Open the block from the opposite side and you will see that the dollar has magically been transferred from the first color ribbons to the crisscrossed second color ribbons.

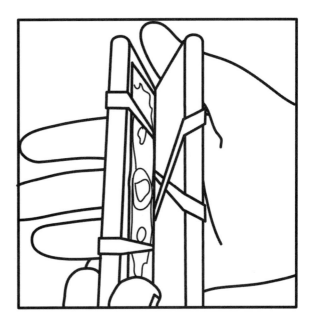

Other Fun Activity Ideas

Juggling

Coin tricks

Build a skateboarding ramp

Build forts out of table and blankets, or bales of straw

Club house

Tree fort

Magic tricks

Build a go-cart

Build a wind skate

String play, such as cat's cradle and witches broom

Table football

Rain makers

Dream catchers

Shadow puppet show

Make homemade musical instruments

Yo-Yo tricks

Dollar bill folding, such as rings, jumping frogs

Tops

Origami

Make a rope swing

Make art projects from autumn leaves

Make sling shots

Home chemistry experiments

Wind chimes

And most important: READ GOOD BOOKS TOGETHER!

About the Author

Michelle has published over twenty articles in peer-reviewed professional journals and has presented her public health research at national and international conferences. Michelle's hobbies include gardening, hiking, cooking, crocheting funky blankets, snow skiing, and jet skiing. She is married to Trent Snow.

Michelle, trent, and their five children, Rachel, Tyler, Austen, Bryson, and Adam, happily reside in Utah. They are kept company by their dog, Lady Isabella of Bromfield, four pet chickens, Hog Mama, Gertie, Argee, and Puffy Checks, and two cats, Señorita Peachalina Gato and Archimedes.

Please visit Michelle's website and blog:

www.michelle-snow.com

www.queenofcommoncents.blogspot.com